7 Powerful Prayers of Friendship with the Holy Spirit

Pius Joseph © Text 2020

TABLE OF CONTENTS

DAY 1

I Need More Than Prayers

Genesis 19:27

> *And Abraham gat up early in the morning to the place where he stood before the Lord:*

Right from Sunday school to our present level of spiritual maturity, the subject of prayer has been sung all along. We hear it in songs. We hear it in church. And in almost everywhere we turn to, we hear people speaking about prayer. It is important, yes we know it. We have also been taught that a powerful Christian is one that prays all the time. There is nothing wrong with that theology because the place of prayer is the place of power. If a believer can learn to pray all the time, no doubt he will be a powerful believer. But being a powerful believer does not make you a friend of the Holy Spirit. There are a lot of powerful believers out there who are making use of the power of the Holy Ghost without actually being his friend.

Samson was fornicating yet he was using the power of the spirit to lift gates and quash the heads of the Philistines.

Judges 16:3

> *And Samson lay till midnight, and arose at midnight, and took the doors of the gate of the city, and the two posts, and went away with them, bar and all, and put them upon his shoulders, and carried them up to the top of an hill that is before Hebron.*

He was setting their fields on fire and destroying everything that they had. What a powerful Samson!

Judges 15:4-6

And Samson went and caught three hundred foxes, and took firebrands, and turned tail to tail, and put a firebrand in the midst between two tails.

5 And when he had set the brands on fire, he let them go into the standing corn of the Philistines, and burnt up both the shocks, and also the standing corn, with the vineyards and olives.

6 Then the Philistines said, Who hath done this? And they answered, Samson, the son in law of the Timnite, because he had taken his wife, and given her to his companion. And the Philistines came up, and burnt her and her father with fire.

Using the power of the Holy Spirit to do exploits without any iota of friendship with the spirit of God. Even if you search through the entire book of judges, there is nowhere it was indicated that Samson had a good friendship with the Holy Spirit or even with God. The only time he offered prayers, was when he was in dire need of water.

Judges 15:18-19

And he was sore athirst, and called on the Lord, and said, Thou hast given this great deliverance into the hand of thy servant: and now shall I die for thirst, and fall into the hand of the uncircumcised?
19 But God clave an hollow place that was in the jaw, and there came water

> *thereout; and when he had drunk, his spirit came again, and he revived: wherefore he called the name thereof En-hakkore, which is in Lehi unto this day.*

Friends, it is possible to have the power of the Holy Ghost without being a friend of the Holy Ghost. A person can get the power of the Holy Spirit by fasting a lot and praying in tongues. If you follow the protocols for getting the power of the spirit, you get the power. But there is a difference between power and friendship. And that is what I intend to show you on this first day.

The Holy Spirit is the gentle personality of the Godhead and requires a higher level of prayer called communion to be able to make him your friend. In all of this, I am not trying to say that prayer is bad. If as a believer you don't pray or take your prayer life very seriously, your life will be predisposed to the attacks of the devil. It is for this reason that we need to pray all the time. As a person, when the Lord gives me grace sometimes I pray for 5 to 10 hours in a day. That is to tell you that I also love praying because I know what it can do to the life of a believer. But when it comes to friendship with the Holy Spirit, you need more than prayer. You need what is called communion with the Holy Ghost.

Sometimes we come into the place of prayer and pray for long hours and when we are done, we leave. Certain things are in the hearts of God which he may want us to know but because we are in a hurry we leave we couldn't.

Whenever you pray in tongues or in the spirit, you have spoken to God. It is also important for God to speak back to you. The communion is not a one-way traffic communication, where one person sits down and talk alone. It is a two-way communication where both individuals are heavily involved in the communication. After you spend some time praying, be quiet let God speak to you too. The Bible says to be still and know that I am God.

Psalms 46:10

*Be still, and know that I am
God: I will be exalted among
the heathen, I will be exalted
in the earth.*

It is in the stillness that you can unravel the heart of God. But when you pray and want to leave the presence of God, your fellowship is incomplete. What completes every fellowship you have with God is communion. It is at the place of communion that God can communicate his heart to you. And when that obligation of communion is not fulfilled, your prayer is incomplete.

Sometimes, we feel that once we fulfil our prayer obligation to God, by praying daily, we have done well. We have prayed in the day as we ought to after all. But we have forgotten that besides prayer, God wants communion with the Holy Spirit. While the place of prayer is the place of revelation, when we add communion to our prayer we can know the deep things of the heart of God. And the only way we can get to company with God is through the Holy Spirit and no one else. The Holy Spirit is the only personality by which our communion with God must take place.

A man who comes to the place of prayer and prays for five hours mainly because he wants something isn't having communion with God but using God. Once the man knows that he has gotten all that he wants from God, off he goes.

Even as human beings we often feel used by men whenever they value our presence only when a need is in sight. The person may not need you but only desires your presence when he has a problem. When an individual is behaving that way, men begin to feel used. They gradually begin to protest solemnly or express concern over the attitude of the individual that is trying to use them.

If the person continues without amending his ways, they begin to avoid his presence, and one day when they see the person coming, they begin to complain maybe he is coming to ask for something again.

The Bible tells us that God created us in his image and likeness. Some of the things that we demonstrate are part of God nature. The same thing happens to God when we try to use him to get what we want. When we pray and spend time with God because a need is in view, we are trying to use him. Such a person can never forge any friendship with the Holy Spirit. His time of prayer that should be used for communion has been turned into a place to give me this or give me that. Which is the reason why it takes more than prayer to develop a friendship with the Holy Spirit? To get to a level where you can be a friend of the Holy Spirit, you have to imbibe the lifestyle of communion.

Communion involves an exchange of verbal or non-verbal communication between two people.

Even if your purpose of praying is to get something from the Lord, ensure that your communion with the Holy Spirit occupies a top spot. You should be able to sit down quietly and hear what God has to say or at least give him some attention. But when you pray and quickly rise from the place of prayer, you haven't communed, you just prayed.

There was a time in my life that I would spend hours, quiet in the place of prayer, listening to the Holy Spirit and all that he would say. Sometimes, it could be before praying in tongues or after I was done praying in the spirit. I would just lay down there in communion with the Holy Ghost. I would lock myself in my room and spend time talking with the Holy Spirit. I later stopped doing that and began to pray alone. Whenever I come into the place of prayer, I won't commune. I would just pray. The Holy Spirit began to remind me of the type of lifestyle of communion that I had. He told me that what he wants from me is communion.

When you communed with God, you can learn a lot of things because the heart of God is communicated during the process of communion. When you have gone into the place of prayer and prayed, you have done your part of talking to God. He also has to talk to you. Whatever means God uses to communicate back to you, yours is to listen to what he has to say whether he says it verbally or not. It could even be by impressing things on your heart or he shows you a vision. It is still communion provided he can talk back to you after you have spoken to him, you have communed.

What I am saying here is not only related to matured believers who can hear the voice of God or discern the various speaking of God. Communion is for all believers in Jesus Christ. There is no categorisation or limitation of who can commune with the Holy Ghost. You can start at the level of your spirituality and develop a friendship with the Holy Spirit through communion. It doesn't matter whether you hear God's voice or not. God can speak to you in different ways. I remember the story of a woman of God, Choo Thomas, who went on to be with the Lord some years back. Before she started hearing the voice of God, she would spend a lot of time with the Lord and commune with him. To her, whether she was hearing the voice of God or not, it never bothered her. One day, God started speaking to her.

The Bible tells us that the ways of a man might be innocent to him, but motives are weighed by the Lord.

Proverbs 16:2

> *All a man's ways seem innocent to him,*
> *but motives are weighed by the Lord.*

(NIV)

He knows when our motive is to spend time with him in communion. He also knows when our motive is to get something from him. If your motive for coming into the presence of God is to commune with him, then there is no way that he won't talk to you. This is one of the secrets of hearing the voice of God. If you can spend time with him in communion, then he will talk to you. If you aren't hearing the voice of God now, you can begin to apply this secret to unlocking his voice in your ears. We will go through Scriptures and examine some men of communion and how they were able to build a life of friendship with the Holy Spirit.

Examples of Scriptural Men of Fellowship

Jesus

He had a life of communion with the Holy Spirit. Did Jesus had the Holy Spirit? Yes, he did. The Bible tells us that he was anointed with the Holy Ghost.

Acts 10:38

> How God anointed Jesus of
> Nazareth with the Holy
> Ghost and with power: who
> went about doing good, and

healing all that were oppressed of the devil; for God was with him.

The Bible says God gave the spirit to Jesus not by measure to him.

John 3:34

For he whom God hath sent speaketh the words of God: for God giveth not the Spirit by measure unto him.

It was the same way that the prophets of old were anointed with the Holy Spirit that Jesus was also anointed. David was anointed to become a king.

1 Sam 16:13

Then Samuel took the horn of oil, and anointed him in

the midst of his brethren: and the Spirit of the Lord came upon David from that day forward. So Samuel rose up, and went to Ramah.

The Bible says the spirit of the Lord came upon him from that day forward. So he had the Holy Spirit. So Jesus had a life of communion. The truth is that prayer can be done anywhere and everywhere. But communion with the Holy Spirit can never be done anywhere and everywhere. It requires a quiet atmosphere where the Holy Ghost and the child of God will have intimacy. Where noise won't interrupt the fellowship. Do you now see why Jesus was always withdrawing from the crowd to have communion with the Holy Spirit.

Mark 6:46

> *And when he had sent them away, he departed into a mountain to pray.*

It wasn't just prayer. It was communion. He knew that if the disciples were to remain with him, they could start one of their arguments, who's the greatest among us? Or a disturbing noise from the ever probing Peter or one of them who wanted to know this or that. Even in the Garden of Gethsemane, Jesus continued with his life of communion up to the last moment.

Matthew 26:39

> *And he went a little further, and fell on his face, and prayed, saying, O my Father,*

if it be possible, let this cup pass from me: nevertheless not as I will, but as thou wilt.

He would have stayed with the disciples to pray alongside them. Or isn't that the best way to have an agreement prayer with the brethren. But he withdrew to a quiet place to pray, to commune with the Holy Ghost, and talk to the Father so that he could receive strength. That is the life of communion that Jesus had which made him forge such unbreakable friendship with the Holy Spirit. You want friendship, then spend time in communion with the Holy Ghost. A heart-to-heart conversation can never take place in a noisy atmosphere. Even Jesus knew that.

Paul the Apostle

Paul the Apostle was speaking to the people of Corinthians who were praying in tongues in a disorderly manner. He told them that I pray in tongues more than you all.

1 Corinthians 14:18-19

> *I thank my God, I speak with tongues more than ye all:*
> *19 Yet in the church I had rather speak five words with my understanding, that by my voice I might teach others also, than ten thousand words in an unknown tongue.*

Then he went ahead to drop a serious revelation about his communion life with the Holy Ghost. He said I would pray in tongues, and I will pray with the understanding also. Telling you that there are times that he just sat down to discuss with the Holy Ghost so that he could understand and know him in a deeper way and manner.

Philippians 3:10

> *That I may know him, and the power of his resurrection, and the fellowship of his sufferings, being made conformable unto his death;*

How was Paul the Apostle able to develop that deep knowledge of God as expressed in the above scripture? Through communion with the Holy Spirit. You can't know Jesus in this present dispensation without communion with the Holy Spirit.

A communion lifestyle of prayer where he and the Holy Ghost just talk all the time. No wonder he was entrusted with such depth of revelation of God, that even Peter confessed that some of the things that Paul the Apostle wrote are hard to understand.

2 Peter 3:16

> *As also in all his epistles, speaking in them of these things; in which are some things hard to be understood, which they that are unlearned and unstable wrest, as they do also the other scriptures, unto their destruction.*

Now, this type of revelation can never be gotten or obtained except in communion with the Holy Spirit.

Peter

Peter, one of the twelve apostles of Jesus Christ also had a life of communion with the Holy Spirit. He had learned the act of communion with the Holy Spirit by seeing what Jesus his master did. All that Jesus did and his life of communion with God left an indelible mark in the life of Peter. So when Jesus was crucified, dead, and buried, and after three days he resurrected, an impartation of the kind of communion life that Jesus led was deposited into the life of Peter. That is why it is very important to know the kind of people you hang around with. If you are always in the company of people who are hungry and passionate about the Holy Ghost, the same kind of hunger and passion will be transferred to you.

In the book of Acts 10: 10-16, we saw that Peter was a man of communion. The Bible recorded the event that transpired as follows:

> On the morrow, as they went on their journey, and drew nigh unto the city, Peter went up upon the housetop to pray about the sixth hour:
> 10 And he became very hungry, and would have eaten: but while they made ready, he fell into a trance,
> 11 And saw heaven opened, and a certain vessel descending unto him, as it had been a great sheet knit at the four corners, and let down to the earth:
> 12 Wherein were all manner of fourfooted beasts of the

earth, and wild beasts, and creeping things, and fowls of the air.

13 And there came a voice to him, Rise, Peter; kill, and eat.

14 But Peter said, Not so, Lord; for I have never eaten any thing that is common or unclean.

15 And the voice spake unto him again the second time, What God hath cleansed, that call not thou common.

16 This was done thrice: and the vessel was received up again into heaven.

Peter was spending time with God on the rooftop of the house when he saw a vision. Through the vision, God was able to communicate to him an important message which he needed to preach to the house of Cornelius. We can say for all intent and purposes, that Peter wasn't praying alone. He was having a communion with the Holy Spirit that was the reason why God was able to talk back to him.

Developing a lifestyle of prayer is good. Yet if friendship with the Holy Ghost is your desire, you must not be a prayer warrior alone. Also, be a communion warrior. It is only when you develop a lifestyle of communion that your friendship with the Holy Spirit can begin to grow.

Elements of Communion

A Quiet Atmosphere

While prayer can take place everywhere and anywhere, communion can only take place in a quiet atmosphere. If you are in a noisy environment, it will be impossible for you to commune with God. That heart-to-heart communication would be interrupted by the noise in the surrounding atmosphere. When Peter wanted to commune with the Holy Spirit we saw in the book of Acts 10:9, that he went on to the rooftop. He was seeking a quiet atmosphere where the Holy Ghost would be able to talk to him.

And as he got that quiet atmosphere, we saw that God spoke to him an indication that it was a communion that he was having with the Holy Ghost. If you are a man who has ignored the place of communion in a quiet ambience, your friendship with the Holy Spirit can never be attained.

Communication

1 Samuel 18:22

> *And Saul commanded his servants, saying, Commune with David secretly, and say, Behold, the king hath delight in thee, and all his servants love thee: now therefore be the king's son in law.*

No communion is ever complete without the vital element of communication. Saul said to commune with David meaning talk to David. Spend some time talking with David not just anywhere, but secretly. How powerful this scripture is. It fully captures how commune should be, there must be some sort of talking.

If it is indeed a true communion, then both parties would have shared either a verbal or non-verbal means of interaction.

Friends, if you go into the presence of the Lord and merely prayed without him communicating with you, you haven't commune. You have communion with the Holy Spirit when he can talk to you and communicate some of the things that are in the heart of God in that season with you.

Patience

No one can ever commune with the Holy Spirit if he is not a man of patience. This is a requirement for communion. After you have prayed and spent time with the Lord, you have to humble yourself for him to talk to you. It may not be immediate, but as you maintain the stillness in his presence, you will begin to hear him. Which accounts for the reason why patience is one of the fruits of the spirit of God. And it is an asset when it comes to communion with the Holy Spirit. It is as a result of impatience that many of us leave the presence of God as if someone is chasing us away. We do not have the patience to wait. Once we have loaded the atmosphere with our tongues or praying in the spirit, we quickly leave as if we have an appointment to catch up outside. This is a great indication of impatience. We cannot wait and hear what God has to say. I still remember a song that was sung when I was a child, "God has something to say, God has something to say, listen, listen, pay full attention for God has something to say."

How beautifully this song captures the vital element of communion. If you can wait, he would speak. And if you can't wait, you won't hear, and he won't speak.

Our generation has been permeated by the spirit of impatience. Everybody is in a hurry going to where I don't know. And if you allow the spirit of impatience into your life that is prominent in our generation, it is going to affect your communion with the Holy Spirit.

Sometimes when you come into the presence of the Lord, you just seat there quietly waiting for him to say something. Men who have understood the secret of communion are some of the greatest friends of the Holy Spirit on the face of the earth. Those who have ignored him, have the Holy Spirit but do not know that they can make him their best friend.

Friends, I know that as you are reading this right now the Holy Spirit is beginning to convict you of your neglect of the place of communion which has affected his friendship with you. When it is time for us to pray, I want you to pray with the whole of your heart so that God can give you the grace to become a man or woman of communion with the Holy Spirit. When that communion has been achieved between you and the Holy Spirit, friendship with the Spirit of God is one of the evidence that we will be seeing out of your life.

Reflection

Psalms 16:7

> *I will bless the Lord, who hath given me counsel: my reins also instruct me in the night seasons.*

Isaiah 1:18

> *Come now, and let us reason together, saith the Lord: though your sins be as scarlet, they shall be as white as snow; though they be red*

> *like crimson, they shall be as*
> *wool.*

Holy Father, it is you who is supposed to use me and not me who is supposed to use you. I plead for mercy in any area that I have desired to make use of you instead of you using me in the name of Jesus.

Heavenly Father, I ask for mercy where I have cared only for my interests without looking at the need for communion with the Holy Spirit. Forgive me Lord and have mercy upon me in the name of Jesus.

Righteous Father, I ask for the grace to develop the fruit of patience so that I can wait in your presence and commune with your spirit in the name of Jesus.

Gracious Father, where I have been hurrying out of your presence every time I come into the place of prayer, I ask for mercy, and I pray that you will help me to stay with you and commune with your spirit in the name of Jesus.

Holy Father, I know that it is not by might, nor by power but by the spirit. Release upon me the grace to develop a life of communion with the Holy Spirit in the name of Jesus.

Heavenly Father, I reject every attempt to develop the culture of this age that is full of impatience in the name of Jesus.

Gracious Father, help me to be a man of the quiet place in the name of Jesus.

Holy Father, in any way that the Holy Spirit has been nudging me to commune with him, but I have neglected the call, I pray that you have mercy upon me in the name of Jesus.

Righteous Father, baptise me with the hunger and thirst for the place of prayer and communion with the Holy Spirit in the name of Jesus.

Holy Father, where the Holy Spirit has been speaking to me in the place of communion but I haven't been able to hear, remove everything that is serving as a blockage of communion in my life in the name of Jesus.

Thank you Holy Father for granting me my petition because I know that from now henceforth, I will become a man of

communion with the Holy Spirit in the name
of Jesus.

DAY 2

Seek my face and not my hand

1 Chronicles 16:11

> *Seek the Lord and his strength, seek his face continually.*

I know that we have discussed this in day one and we have prayed about communion with the Holy Spirit. However, we are going to discuss this subject matter from a different light of scripture. The face of a man is the point of recognition. If the facial features of a man can be known anywhere that you see that man, he is easily identifiable. Through the face of that man, whenever you see him, you will just say, is that not brother so or sister so that is coming from that walkway? The reason for the easy identification of the person is as a result of his facial features. It is through the face of that man that we were able to know him. Although it is possible as a result of technological advancement to know somebody through biometrics and fingerprint identification, the old way of knowing people through their faces is one of the best whenever the technology fails.

It is through the face of a man that you can know who he is. It is also through the face of the man that you can identify him from a distance. So whenever a man is truly seeking the face of the Lord, he intends to know him.

Some of the prayers we pray claiming to seek the face of the Lord are prayers of selfishness. Someone will say, I am seeking the face of the Lord for his anointing to be poured upon my life. But his intention is not to seek the face of the LORD to know him and walk with the Spirit. It is to consume the anointing of the Lord upon his lust.

Some of our fasting and prayers are also born out of an impure intention. Someone would tell you I am fasting and seeking the face of the Lord for a new car. What is the purpose of the car? So that he can use it to show his neighbour that he too has a new car. That fasting and prayer is not for seeking the face of the Lord to know him and walk with the Spirit, but to satisfy a selfish desire. I am not saying praying for a car is bad! Yet our greatest desire to seek the face of the Lord should be moved by one lone purpose of knowing the Holy Spirit and having a friendship with him. Then car and other things can begin to follow us. When you are a friend of the Holy Ghost, you don't pray for every need. As you desperately pursue the Holy Spirit in a tight friendship, God will give you all the things that you haven't been praying for. And this is in line with scriptural truth we are to seek first God's Kingdom. And is the pursuit of the Holy Spirit a part of God's kingdom? I will answer a hundred per cent yes.

Matthew 6:33

But seek ye first the kingdom of God, and his righteousness; and all these things shall be added unto you.

We've simply reversed the order. We are chasing things instead of chasing the most important things in life. The Bible says we should seek after the kingdom of God and all the things of life will be added to us. Instead, we are chasing the things of the world and waiting for the things of God to be added unto us. And as long as we don't pursue the most important things of life, which is the kingdom of God and the friendship with the Holy Spirit, we will continue to have fewer believers who will enjoy a quality friendship with the Holy Spirit. Nothing can be further from the truth. If we do what Jesus did if we do what Paul the apostle did, and if we do what Peter did, a good friendship with the Holy Spirit will be our portion.

That is the reason why we have so many prayer warriors who pray for hours every day but have been unable to develop a friendship with the Holy Spirit.

Most of us are culprits of seeking the face of the Lord for personal aggrandizement. Our desires are embedded in our prayers. And when we pray like that, friendship with the Holy Spirit will continue to remain a mirage.

Also, a man who is out rightly seeking the hand of the Lord is one who is after what God can give and not what God is to him. For that man, the sole purpose of his prayers is to be able to get what is in the hand of God. He is after the hand of God and not the face of God. For such persons, they can never become a friend of the Holy Spirit.

When we seek the face of the Lord from a genuine intention of knowing him, we will be able to know the Holy Spirit and create a bond of friendship with him.

Reflection

Acts 17:27

> *That they should seek the Lord, if haply they might feel after him, and find him, though he be not far from every one of us:*

James 4:8

Draw nigh to God, and he will draw nigh to you. Cleanse your hands, ye sinners; and purify your hearts, ye double minded.

Holy Father, I ask for mercy where I have sought your face for what you can do and not for who you are in the name of Jesus.

Heavenly Father, I asked that you deliver me from every selfish intention of seeking your face so that I can get something from your hand in the name of Jesus.

Gracious Father, help me to seek your face and not your hand so that I will know you by your spirit and create a friendship with you.

Righteous Father, I ask that you align my desire for the right purpose of knowing you in the name of Jesus.

Holy Father, I ask that as I seek your face may I know the Holy Spirit and develop a friendship with him in the name of Jesus.

Gracious Father, anything that I need to know whenever I seek your face that will build my friendship with the Holy Spirit, I pray that you will teach me in the name of Jesus.

Righteous Father, help me to be able to seek your face all the time and not your hand in the name of Jesus.

Heavenly Father, I ask that you draw me close to you in an everlasting friendship with the Holy Spirit as I seek your face in the name of Jesus.

Holy Father, release upon me the passion to seek your face with the pure intention in the name of Jesus.

Thank you Holy Father because I know that from now henceforth I will begin to seek your face and not your hand in all areas of my life in the name of Jesus.

DAY 3

I Desire to Know You

Psalms 119:20

> *My soul is overwhelmed with endless longing for your regulations.*

It may interest you to know that even though God is our creator, he still wants to know us. The Bible tells us that the heart of man is deceitful above all things. For God to be able to know man, he carries out searching in the heart of that man.

Psalms 139:23-24

*Search me, O God, and know
my heart: try me, and know
my thoughts:
24 And see if there be any
wicked way in me, and lead
me in the way everlasting.*

He searches the heart to know what is in it.

Jeremiah 17:9

*The heart is deceitful above
all things, and desperately
wicked: who can know it?*

Even though God knew the children of Israelites before they left Egypt, God had to subject them to a series of test to know what is in their hearts. God even said I will do this to know if they will keep my commandments. Does that mean God does not know them? He knows them. But the heart of man is the central focus of God. That is why at salvation, God works on the heart. When the heart is renewed, the man is changed. What is in your heart towards God?

If God wants to know the heart of a man, he allows several things to happen to that man. And through what has befallen the man, he will be able to know what is in the heart of that man. Job was subject to a severe test because God wanted to know what is in his heart. At the beginning of the test, Job was busy praising God and giving Him thanks. But as everything got intensified, he opened his mouth and curse the day of his birth.

Friends, some of the things that God allows to come through your path, is a way to test what is your heart. If your attitude towards him is poor, it will affect your ability to build a friendship with the spirit of God. God's instrument for testing the heart of a man is test, trials, and the temptations he allows to come to us. And your attitude when these negative events befall you is very critical. I have never seen a man who has a bad attitude towards the trials that have come to his life that was able to build a friendship with the Holy Spirit except God shows him mercy. The attitude of your heart is very important to you and God. It is important to God because he uses the trials and test to know you. It is also important to you because the trials and test that come to you and your subsequent attitude can affect the relationship you can build with the Holy Spirit. It is for this reason that Paul the Apostle said in the book of Acts 24:16 that he exercised himself to have a conscience that is void of offence towards God and towards man:

Acts 24:16

> *And herein do I exercise myself, to have always a conscience void of offence toward God, and toward men.*

Friends, whenever you begin to experience diverse trials and temptation come your way, it is God who is allowing it for knowing you. While you do not control what will come your way, you can control your responses to those events. And how you respond to these events, can affect your relationship with God.

We need to be careful with the way we respond to events when things are not going our way. The Holy Spirit is the closest personality to us among the Godhead. So whenever we demonstrate any negative attitude, he's always the first person to receive it from us. It is for this reason that we need to be careful with the kind of attitude we demonstrate whenever a negative event happens to us. Before the Holy Spirit can draw you closer to himself in a bond of friendship, you must be tested. In the same way that God tested Abraham to determine what is in his heart that is the same way, you will be tested too. And after every test, there is a promotion. May the Lord help our attitude in times of trials and temptations in the name of Jesus.

Reflection

Isaiah 26:9

> *With my soul have I desired thee in the night; yea, with my spirit within me will I seek thee early: for when thy judgments are in the earth, the inhabitants of the world will learn righteousness.*

James 1:2-4

> *My brethren, count it all joy when ye fall into divers temptations;*

> *3 Knowing this, that the trying of your faith worketh patience.*
> *4 But let patience have her perfect work, that ye may be perfect and entire, wanting nothing.*

Holy Father, I ask for mercy in any area of my life that I have demonstrated a negative attitude towards the things that have happened to me in the name of Jesus.

Heavenly Father, I also pray for mercy where I have failed to take advantage of the test and trials that come my way without knowing that it was meant for my promotion to a close walk with you in the name of Jesus.

Gracious Father, I know that without you I can do nothing. I pray that when difficult moments come my path supply me with enough grace to demonstrate the right attitude towards you in the Mighty name of Jesus.

Holy Father, I pray for the grace to pass every test that you have allowed me to pass through in the name of Jesus.

Gracious Father, I pray for the baptism of the consciousness of the fact that my attitude will affect the Holy Spirit more so that I will be careful with the kind of attitude I show whenever things go wrong in my life in the name of Jesus.

Heavenly Father, I know that you are faithful and you will never allow any trial or temptation to come upon me that is greater than my capacity to bear. I pray that you will make a way for me to pass every trial to promotion in the name of Jesus.

Gracious Father, I pray that you will help me to understand the fact that every time a trial comes my way it is an opportunity to draw closer to the Holy Spirit in friendship in the name of Jesus.

Thank you Holy Father for the perfect attitude which you have given to me to demonstrate always so that my actions do not affect the Holy Spirit in the name of Jesus.

DAY 4

Let Me, Minister, through You

Ephesians 4:11-13

And he gave some, apostles; and some, prophets; and some, evangelists; and some, pastors and teachers;
12 For the perfecting of the saints, for the work of the ministry, for the edifying of the body of Christ:
13 Till we all come in the unity of the faith, and of the knowledge of the Son of God, unto a perfect man, unto the measure of the stature of the fulness of Christ:

The reason why God is preparing us for what is ahead of us is to equip us for service. The Holy Spirit will never ask you to do anything he won't help you do. If he is asking you to do anything it is because he has already given you the capacity to do that thing. What the Holy Spirit is looking for is an available vessel that will agree to do what is in the heart of God. You see all the gifts of God that are upon your life, whether it is the gift of healing, working miracles, interpretation of tongues, prophecy, et cetera God has given it to you so that the Holy Spirit will use those gifts as instruments of ministration to others.

The Holy Spirit is not asking you to go and heal the sick, but he will do the healing of the sick through your life. There is nothing that God has asked us to do that he hasn't given us the capacity to do it. Whenever God is making a demand, there is already existing capacity.

The Holy Spirit requires vessels that he will use. Once he finds a vessel that is willing to cooperate with him so that he can minister through that vessel to others, the friendship will be forged. The challenge is that many of us are crying for friendship with the Holy Spirit but we don't want to make ourselves available for Him to use us to touch the lives of others around us. It is the available that will be the friend of the Holy Ghost. It is not even the gifted. It is also not the most intelligent. It is only those who have made themselves available for the Holy Spirit to pass through them and touch others that will be his friend.

The Spirit is calling you today to allow him to use the gifts he has deposited into your life as a tool for touching the lives of people. Making yourself available for him to do what he pleases with your life, is the first step towards building a lasting friendship with the Holy Spirit. Those who can obey the leading of the Holy Spirit for him to use the gift in their lives to minister to others will be able to make him their friend.

I want you to carry out a careful examination of your life and the type of gifts that the Holy Spirit has given you. And ask yourself this pertinent question, am I allowing the Holy Spirit to use the gifts he has given me to minister to the life of others? If you haven't been allowing him to use the gifts he has given you to minister to people, then friendship with the Holy Spirit is impossible. You can't deny him the use of your life and expect to be his friend. It doesn't work that way.

If you are asking yourself, well I don't even know the gifts that the Holy Spirit has given me. You are asking this question because you haven't spent time knowing him. If you spend time with the Holy Spirit, the gift of the spirit will surely manifest in your life and it will be easier for you to identify them.

You see some of the little instructions that the Holy Spirit gives us here and there, is to cultivate the gift he has given us so that when he makes a demand for it, we will make it available for him to use and touch the lives of people around us. Which is why every believer must cooperate with the Holy Spirit in every area of his life. When he gives you instructions, obey them. The instructions of today are part of the preparation for making you a tool for his use tomorrow. When we struggle with him and refused to allow him the use of our life, he can't be our friend.

Whenever I hear people say, it is my life I can do whatever I want to do with it. I know that they are speaking out of ignorance. What is it that a man has that was not given to him? Is it the breath in your nostrils? The different parts of the body you possess? Your job? Your car? And all your charitable possessions! All of these things were graciously given to you by God. And whenever he placed a demand on them, your sole duty is to release what he has given to you for his use. It is not for you to begin to struggle with him.

God is an investor. He invested in the life of man by giving him the best comforter that the world has ever known – The Holy Spirit. And no investor won't want to profit from the fruits of his investment. God has invested so much into your life by giving you the Holy Spirit and the different gifts that he has given you. A time is coming that he will want to use those gifts as a tool for ministration to others.

Another aspect of allowing the Holy Spirit to use you is for people to feel God through your life. God is aware that without the fruit of the spirit showing forth in our lives, we won't be different from the people of the world. The world says, love those who love you. Be kind to those who are kind to you but that is not the standard of God. It is through the help of the Holy Spirit and the fruit of the spirit in our lives that we can show love and kindness to people who don't deserve it. When we allow people to feel the spirit of God through our lives, we are indirectly ministering to them. Sometimes we don't need to open our mouths to talk, our actions can speak louder than our words. And some of these actions are communicated via the fruit of the spirit. The only thing we need to do is to cooperate with the Holy Spirit so that he develops those fruit of the spirit in our lives to use them to touch the lives of people around us.

Will you release yourself to him so that he can use you? I will allow you to think about this question through and answer it when you are meditating. I pray that the Lord will help us not to hold ourselves back when it is time for him to use us in the name of Jesus.

Reflection

Isaiah 6:8

> *Also I heard the voice of the Lord, saying, Whom shall I send, and who will go for us? Then said I, Here am I; send me.*

1 Samuel 12:24

> *Only fear the Lord, and serve him in truth with all your heart: for consider how great things he hath done for you.*

Holy Father, whatever gift that the Holy Spirit has released into my life I pray that may the gifts begin to manifest in the name of Jesus.

Heavenly Father, I ask that you help me not to hold myself back whenever the Lord makes a demand upon anything that he has given to me in the name of Jesus.

Gracious Father, help me to make myself available for your use in the name of Jesus.

Righteous Father, anything that is preventing me from making myself available for your use, I pray that in your mercy you will remove that thing in the name of Jesus.

Holy Father, I pray for the grace to cooperate with your Spirit so that he will be able to pass through me to reach out to others in the name of Jesus.

Heavenly Father, anything in my life that is preventing the Holy Spirit from passing through me to reach out to others, I ask that in your mercy you will remove that thing in the name of Jesus.

Heavenly Father, I surrender my life to you and I ask that you use it for whatever purpose that you please in the name of Jesus.

Gracious Father, where I have withhold my life in the past, today I release myself to you in the name of Jesus.

Righteous Father, as I release myself to you and allow the Holy Spirit to minister through me, may that lead to the development of a good friendship with the Holy Spirit in the name of Jesus.

Holy Father, where my friendship with the Holy Spirit has been suffering because I struggled to allow the Holy Spirit to use me for your glory, deliver me from the life of such struggle in the name of Jesus.

Thank you Holy Father for how the Holy Spirit will begin to use me from now henceforth. I know that as a result of this, my friendship with the Holy Spirit will begin to grow to a new level in the name of Jesus.

DAY 5

Stop Taking My Spirit for Granted

Proverbs 16:3

> *Commit thy works unto the Lord, and thy thoughts shall be established.*

Yesterday, we considered the important issue of allowing God to minister through us so that the Holy Spirit can become a friend. Today, we are going to delve into a different subject matter that can either make or mar our friendship with the Holy Spirit. My prayer is that after we have studied for today and prayed the prayers contained at the end of the chapter, we will become serious with the Holy Spirit in the name of Jesus.

Many a believer do not have a problem with honouring the Father. A lot of believers also do not have a problem with honouring Jesus. However, when it comes to the Holy Spirit, we don't care. The reason for this lack of reverence for the Holy Spirit is because of the distorted way in which he has been presented to us. After all, if the Holy Spirit is only a dove to you or fire or water or even a wind, how would you be able to honour him effectively and not take him for granted?

When God created us and wanted man to carry the same power that created the earth, he put in us the Holy Spirit. So that we will be able to be like him in every perspective. When God wanted us to carry the same power that resurrected Jesus from the grave, he gave us the Holy Spirit. If the Holy Spirit is an important personality that his presence was needed at creation, because the Bible tells us that the spirit of God was hovering above the waters to pave way for the creation, then he is not a personality that we should take for granted. In the same way that we reverence God the Father, and God the Son, that is the same way that we are supposed to reverence the Holy Spirit. After all, he is also God. And not a God with a small letter g.

If you think that the Holy Spirit will continue to remain in your life while taking him for granted, you will be surprised to see that there are a lot of people that the Holy Spirit has left them. It is because God does not want anyone to take his Spirit for granted that is the reason why a man can sin against the Father he could be forgiven. He can sin against the Son and obtain mercy. But there is a type of sin that a man can commit against the Holy Spirit that he won't be forgiven. That is the blasphemy of the Holy Spirit. The reason for this is simple, God does not want us to take the Holy Spirit for granted.

It is time to scrutinise your life and begin to examine areas of your life that you have taken the Holy Spirit for granted. Are there instructions that he has given you which you never took seriously? Are there things that the Holy Spirit has been nudging you for months and you simply refused to comply with the nudging? What is it that the Holy Spirit has been impressing on your heart which was never taken seriously? If you are taking the Holy Spirit for granted, I can tell you that your friendship with him will never grow. You can pray from now until the time that Jesus comes if you do not begin to reverence the Holy Spirit, he can't be your friend.

Recently, I began to take personal responsibility in my life for all the things that the Holy Spirit has commanded me to do. I'm not speaking about outright disobedience or rebellion. I am speaking about things that the Holy Spirit may gently drop on the canvas of my heart which I may forget, and I get busy doing other things. I know that it can hinder good friendship with the Holy Spirit. So I started to take responsibility for that in my life to ensure I do not take those things for granted. My prayer is that God will help us not to take his Spirit for granted so that we can be his bosom friend.

Reflection

Proverbs 3:5-7

Trust in the Lord with all thine heart; and lean not

unto thine own understanding.
6 In all thy ways acknowledge him, and he shall direct thy paths.
7 Be not wise in thine own eyes: fear the Lord, and depart from evil.

Psalms 37:5

Commit thy way unto the Lord; trust also in him; and he shall bring it to pass.

Holy Father, forgive me for all the times that I have taken your Spirit for granted in the name of Jesus.

Heavenly Father, where ever I have failed to give due reverence to the Holy Spirit as I ought to, I ask for mercy in the name of Jesus.

Gracious Father, in every area of my life that I have not taken seriously the dealing of the Holy Spirit, I ask for mercy in the name of Jesus.

Righteous Father, I asked that you will deliver me from every attitude of the heart that will not take the Holy Spirit seriously in the name of Jesus.

Holy Father, I humble myself before you at this moment and I asked that you will help me to give the Holy Spirit his rightful place in my life in the name of Jesus.

Heavenly Father, baptise me with the special grace to accord deserving respect to the Holy Spirit in the name of Jesus.

Gracious Father, whenever that I have been disobedient to the leading of the Holy Spirit I ask for mercy in the name of Jesus.

Righteous Father, anything that the Holy Spirit has been telling me to do which I have refused to do, show me mercy and help me to obey now in the name of Jesus.

Heavenly Father, as I begin to take your spirit seriously, may that create a deep friendship between me and him in the name of Jesus.

Holy Father, as I begin to give the Holy Spirit the due honour that he deserves, I ask that in your mercy let that honour create a bond of friendship between me and the Holy Spirit in the name of Jesus.

Righteous Father, as I begin to see the Holy Spirit as you see him, I ask in your mercy that my friendship with the Holy Spirit will grow to a whole new level in the name of Jesus.

Holy Father, Jesus is my ultimate example. I know that while he was walking on the face of the earth, he always showed honour to your spirit. I pray that I will be able to walk in that same grace that Jesus enjoyed when he was on earth because you have said in your word that we should look unto Jesus who is the author and finisher of our faith in the name of Jesus.

Thank you Holy Father because I know from today the habit of taking the Holy Spirit for granted has ceased permanently in my life in the name of Jesus.

DAY 6

Do Not Ignore Me

Matthew 6:33

> *But seek ye first the kingdom of God, and his righteousness; and all these things shall be added unto you.*

What we have gone through yesterday is an important subject matter. If you haven't prayed the prayers of yesterday as you ought to, I will encourage you to go back to it again before you continue with the prayers for day six. The issue of taking the Holy Spirit for granted has stunted the friendship growth of many believers in the earth. It is impossible to take someone for granted and expect to enjoy the best of their friendship.

Today we are going to handle something very critical to building a lasting friendship with the Holy Spirit on the earth. Before we go on, I will draw huge reference from the Bible in the book of Numbers 22:18 which states as follows:

Numbers 22:18

> *But Balaam, in answer; said to the servants of Balak, Even if Balak gave me his house full of silver and gold, it would not be possible for me to do anything more or less than the orders of the Lord my God.*
>
> (BBE)

Although the Scripture under reference is speaking about Balaam, and his subsequent love for the wages of unrighteousness, what I am paying attention to in that verse of the Bible is the smallest of matters. And because we have failed to recognise the role of the Holy Spirit in the smallest of matters, our friendship with him has been affected in one way or the other. It is never a wise decision to ignore the important role that the Holy Spirit plays in our daily lives.

Unfortunately, we are so fast in our generation that when we wake up sometimes, our hearts are already outside our houses. Without recognising the fact that we needed to invite the Holy Spirit to direct our day. It is a deliberate and conscious effort that we need to make so that the Holy Spirit can take charge of our day. He is interested in the smallest of matters in our lives. I remember sometimes that the Holy Spirit will decide the kind of clothes I should wear when I want to go out. He decides which route I should pass through. What I should eat when I want to grab a quick lunch. The Holy Spirit is interested in everything that we do from the tiniest of matters to the biggest if only we will invite him to take charge. And as we allow Him to lead us in our daily lives, our friendship with him begins to experience dramatic growth.

Friends, I am calling you to practice a kind of new life that you may not have been indulging in. That you should invite the Holy Spirit to lead you in your day. Before you go out of your house, kneel and pray so that the Holy Spirit can guide you. If you ignore the decision of the Holy Spirit in the smallest of matters, why would you want to invite him in the biggest? When you are already aware that he is interested in both. No matter how big it is or no matter how small it is.

The Bible says in the book of Proverbs 3:5-6:

> *Trust in the Lord with all thine heart; and lean not unto thine own understanding.*
> *6 In all thy ways acknowledge him, and he shall direct thy paths.*

7 Be not wise in thine own eyes: fear the Lord, and depart from evil.

It is a call to all believers to acknowledge the Lord in all that we do. And once we can satisfy the requirement of acknowledging him in everything even in the smallest of matters, he will direct our paths. The more we increase the involvement of the Holy Spirit in our day-to-day activities, the more of his friend we will enjoy in our lives.

I pray that the Lord will help us not to ignore the need for the involvement of the Holy Spirit in our day-to-day lives in the name of Jesus.

Reflection

John 14:26

> *But the Comforter, which is the Holy Ghost, whom the Father will send in my name, he shall teach you all things, and bring all things to your remembrance, whatsoever I have said unto you.*

Revelation 22:17

> *And the Spirit and the bride say, Come. And let him that heareth say, Come. And let him that is athirst come. And whosoever will, let him take the water of life freely.*

Holy Father, I pray for the grace that will help me to begin my day with the Holy Spirit in the name of Jesus.

Heavenly Father, whenever that I have ignored the need of the Holy Spirit and began my day, I ask you for mercy in the name of Jesus.

Righteous Father, release upon me the grace to acknowledge the Holy Spirit in the smallest of matters in my life in the name of Jesus.

Gracious Father, you have said in your word that without you, I can do nothing. Help me to recognise this fact that without your spirit in my daily life, I can do nothing in the name of Jesus.

Heavenly Father, I pray that from today the Holy Spirit will begin to guide me from the beginning of my day until the end as I invite him to do so in the name of Jesus.

Holy Father, whatever it is that is preventing me from seeking the help of the Holy Spirit daily help me to work on it in the name of Jesus.

Righteous Father, as I involve the Holy Spirit more and more in my day, let it lead to a greater friendship with him in the name of Jesus.

Gracious Father, may the fingerprint of the Holy Spirit become evident in every area of my life as I go about my daily activities in the name of Jesus.

Righteous Father, I pray that as a Holy Spirit direct my path in smallest matters daily, release upon me the grace to obey those directions in the name of Jesus.

Thank you Holy Father for the grace you have given unto me from now henceforth to seek the involvement of the Holy Spirit in my daily life. This will mark a turning point in my friendship with him in the name of Jesus.

DAY 7

Never Be Tired

Psalm 121:1-3

> *I will lift up mine eyes unto the hills, from whence cometh my help.*
> *2 My help cometh from the Lord, which made heaven and earth.*
> *3 He will not suffer thy foot to be moved: he that keepeth thee will not slumber.*

Friendship with the Holy Spirit is not mere talk, it is hard work. To build a friendship with the Holy Spirit, you must continue to work on your relationship with him. It is not something you do one day and stops. You must give attention to that particular area of your spirituality all the days of your life. One of the greatest hindrances of man is the lack of desire to go all the way until a particular goal has been achieved. You may have already been doing much, working on your relationship with the Holy Spirit but it hasn't started producing fruits yet. It is not for you to stop all the efforts you have put in.

Friends, you do not have to stop now. This is not the time to give up on your relationship with the Holy Spirit. No house was ever built in one day. Even if the house was built in a day, it took time and process before it was eventually completed. Your relationship with the Holy Spirit will not just blossom because you put a little effort. If that is your testimony, we bless God that your little effort has changed your friendship with the Holy Spirit. But in most cases, it takes time and a consistent effort.

It is just like the word of God as the Bible tells us in the book of Luke 13:18-19:

> *Then said he, Unto what is the kingdom of God like? and whereunto shall I resemble it?*
> *19 It is like a grain of mustard seed, which a man took, and cast into his garden; and it grew, and waxed a great tree; and the fowls of the air lodged in the branches of it.*

The sower went ahead to plant the seed. It took time for the seed to grow through the various stages of photosynthesis and germination. It grew until it became a big tree where the birds of the air find it a good nesting place. All of these took place in the process of time. If the farmer had given up when the seed was in the ground going through the process of germination. Would he have seen a tree that the birds of the air will come and put their nests? Certainly, no! It was the resolve and the will of the farmer to continue to take care of the plant that resulted in a big tree that became a place where the bets of the air constructed their nests.

Friends, you might have read several of our books on how to build a friendship with the

Holy Spirit, and prayed all the prayers contained there. It is also possible that you have read several books on the subject of the Holy Spirit and how to make him your friend. You've also been studying your Bible to know the Holy Spirit more. Nothing may be happening now, but something will be happening later and everybody will see the results of your investment into your friendship with the Holy Spirit. Do not give up now!

The Bible tells us that whatever a man sows, that is what that man is going to reap. You have been sowing into your friendship with the Holy Spirit, you will reap nothing other than being the closest friend of the Holy Spirit. It isn't possible to plant apples in the garden and reap mangoes. If what you have planted is an investment towards your friendship with the Holy Spirit that is what you will reap.

Friends, I just want to encourage you that the development of friendship with the Holy Spirit may take a while, but if you have been working on it, then you are on the right path. I assure you that very soon, your friendship with the Holy Spirit will blossom beyond your imagination. Do not lose hope continue to do what you've been doing all this while. Your investment and efforts towards building a friendship with the Holy Spirit are not in vain. The Bible tells us in the book of 1 Corinthians 15:58:

Therefore, my beloved brethren, be ye stedfast, unmoveable, always abounding in the work of the Lord, forasmuch as ye know that your labour is not in vain in the Lord.

You've laboured into your friendship with the Holy Spirit that labour is not in vain. You will surely reap if you do not faint and continue what you have been doing. I pray that the Lord will help us in this area in the name of Jesus.

Reflection

Joshua 1:9

I have commanded you, 'Be strong and courageous!

*Don't tremble or be terrified,
because the Lord your God is
with you wherever you go."'*

Isaiah 41:10

*Don't be afraid, because I am
with you.
Don't be intimidated; I am
your God.
I will strengthen you.
I will help you.
I will support you with my
victorious right hand.*

Holy Father, in any area of my life that I have been trying to build a relationship with the Holy Spirit and discouragement sets in, I pray for your mercy in the name of Jesus.

Heavenly Father, I make demands for the grace to continue to work on my friendship with the Holy Spirit in the name of Jesus.

Glorious Father, you have said in your word that whatever a man sows, that is what he shall reap. As I have sowed into my friendship with the Holy Spirit, let me reap a solid friendship with the Holy Spirit in the name of Jesus.

Righteous Father, help me to continue to remember that my labour in building a friendship with the Holy Spirit is not in vain in the name of Jesus.

Holy Father, where I have stopped building my friendship with the Holy Spirit, I ask for the grace to pick up from where I have stopped and continued in the name of Jesus.

Thank you Holy Father for the mighty grace that you have supplied to me to continue to build my friendship with the Holy Spirit. I know that my labour is not in vain and it will produce results that will take my friendship with the Holy Spirit to the next level in the name of Jesus.

Thank you Holy Father for all the prayers I have prayed from day one to day seven, to you be all the glory and the honour in the name of Jesus.

Important Decision

If you are reading this book and you are not saved, pray this prayer after me:

Lord Jesus, I come before you today. I give you my heart. I give you my all. Come into my life. Become my Lord and saviour. Deliver me from the power of sin. Help me to live for you forever, in Jesus name.

Our Books

1.   Restraining Decrees through Courtroom Prayers: Courts of Heaven Orders for Victory & Breakthroughs

2.   Python Spirit: Complete Deliverance from the Python Spirit with Powerful Prayers

3.   The Courts of Heaven: Prayers that Open the Courts of Heaven for Healing and Deliverance

4.   Powerful Prayers for Your Adult Children: How to Pray for Your Children and Secure their Future

5.   Praying for My Future Husband:How to Pray for Your Husband and Enjoy A Godly Marriage

17.   Prayers that Destroy Infirmities & Diseases: Powerful Prayers that bring Healing to the Sick

18.   Courtroom Prayers: Prayers And Declarations in the Courts of Heaven For Victory, Breakthrough, and Deliverance (Free E-Book

19.   How to make the Holy Ghost Your Closest Friend (Book 2) (Free-Ebook)

20.   The Keys to Fervent Prayer: The Prayer Warrior Guide to Praying Always

21.   Interpretation of Tongues: Be Filled with the Spirit, Unlock Speaking in Tongues & Know What You Are Praying

113

115

* 9 7 9 8 6 4 7 0 5 6 3 6 8 *